WORD

"O.G. Rev is a prophet of the streets. His church has no walls. You can find him walking around with that Bible in Oakland, California, one of the most dangerous cities in North America. There is no secret agenda with him like there is with a lot of these arm chair activists and misleading leaders out here. When you look at Rev, what you see is what you get. He is a man of God. Rev is for the people.

O.G. Rev takes his message to places where most of these pastors wouldn't think about going, and he's going to reach out to the real folks out here — the kind that a whole lot of church people would run from. How do I feel about this book? God loves the people who live in the hood where the stray bullets fly. God loves our brothers and sisters who are locked down. God sees the tears of the mothers who have lost their children to gun violence. There are prayers for all of those folks in this book. Who else could have written it but Rev?"

– Jack Bryson, founding member of the
 Oscar Grant Foundation, union organizer,
 community activist

"Did you know that slavery still exists in America? The San Francisco Bay is a well-known hub for human trafficking which is actually slavery by a more socially acceptable name. I have given my life to fight this curse. Along the way, I have met a number of grassroots soldiers who walk the streets at ground level; O.G. Rev is one of them. He knows the harsh streets of Oakland and is present in them as a minister of the Gospel. May these prayers he's written be used of God to heal you."

– *Vanessa Marie Johnson Russell, Executive Director, Love Never Fails, human trafficking abolitionist*

"Harry comes with a perspective and experience you only get from being close to the streets and those who have been cast aside. He chooses to walk in true agape love in a time and place that so many walk in fear. Harry's words bring to life the experiences of so many fallen soilders and heros of the many forgotten communities that he moves through. His words in *When the Struggle is Real* help to make a connection from real darkness to redemption — darkness that people have known and that Harry has truly taken the time to understand and articulate to the world."

– *Nola Brantley, Executive Director of Nola Brantley Speaks*

WHEN THE STRUGGLE IS REAL

O.G. REV'S HIP HOP PRAYERS & MEDITATIONS

REV. HARRY LOUIS WILLIAMS II
AUTHOR OF "STRAIGHT OUTTA EAST OAKLAND"

SOUL SHAKER PUBLISHING
OAKLAND, CALIFORNIA

When the Struggle is Real
© 2019 Harry Louis Williams, II

All rights reserved. No part of this book may be reproduced in any form or by any electronic or mechanical means, including information storage and retrieval systems, without permission in writing from the publisher, except by a reviewer who may quote brief passages in a review.

Soul Shaker Publishing
Oakland, California
www.IAmOGRev.com

Cover and interior design:
Tamara Dever, TLC Book Design, TLCBookDesign.com

Front cover photo: © Depositphotos.com/SIphotographyStark
Praising man, last page: © Depositphotos.com/slonme

ISBN: 978-0-9789133-2-8

THIS BOOK IS DEDICATED TO:

About a year ago, I was at a church dinner when Reverend Allie Tanner, a friend I'd attended seminary school with, recited a poem to me. It was a prayer that I'd written for her twenty years earlier when she'd tragically lost her sister. I had completely forgotten about that poem. Two decades later, however, she knew it word-for-word. I think it was that night that the idea for this book was born as I listened to her flawlessly recite those words. I would not only write a book of prayers, but a book of prayers that rhymed.

This also goes out to Ms. Irma McDaniel, my second mother, who has been telling me to write a book of prayers for the past 15 years; and to my friend, Ms. Angela Wells Kidd, who told me the same thing.

To my dear friend Tamara Dever of TLC Book Design, whom God has used to bless my hood ministry so dramatically. To Dana, whose editorial services were a blessing to this project.

This book is dedicated to all of the people whom I met along the way who are now incarcerated. This book is written to an underworld hood figure in Oakland, CA. He doesn't know me, but I've seen him several times and with all of his street fame and money, he looks like the most unhappy individual I've ever seen. Perhaps somewhere along the line, he'll pick up this book and find hope.

Finally, this book is dedicated to the founding fathers and mothers of hip-hop.

Love y'all,
"O.G. Rev."

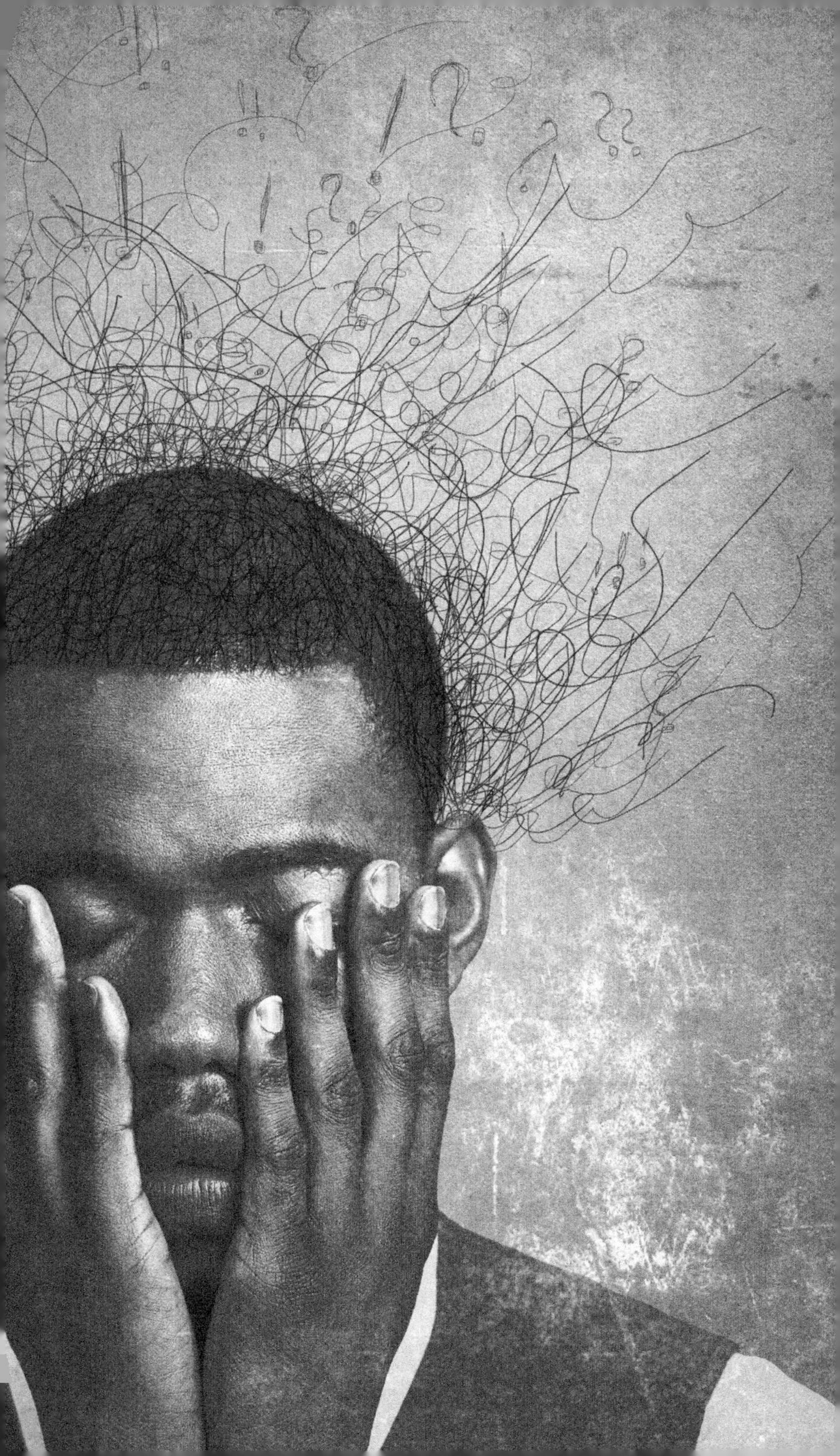

INTRODUCTION

As a minister, I serve people who have been caught up in every kind of hood drama imaginable. I have sat down and prayed with people who were in flight from hit men. I have served people who, as children, saw horrendous things that no human being should ever see. I have ministered to people raised in the monster factory by the monsters. I have laid hands on people serving life because they pulled that trigger. I have prayed with people whose children were slaughtered. They all have one thing in common: God loves them.

Some of these folks are afraid of prayer because they don't know the right words to say. In reality, God isn't sitting there with a dictionary and magic marker, making a red X when you slip and say a slang word. It doesn't work like that. God values authenticity and truth.

What you hold in your hands is a collection of hood prayers. There are prayers for people who can't make the rent. There are prayers for people behind bars. There are no "thees" or "thous" in here. These are real prayers for people in real situations. I pray that they bless you.

– Harry Williams II

PRAYER FOR MY LOVED ONES IN THE STREETS

Lord, they about counting hundreds not just ones;
They don't go to work with shovels, they use guns.
A fool who messes with their bread soon will get buried.
Police lights in the rear view but they ain't worried;

If the lawyer can't kill it, they can do the time.
This is the life they live, dollars made from dimes;
Laying down anything that offers them resistance.
But, oh God, what an awful waste of existence!
Born with so many gifts, and given so many talents,
But choose to live with your life twirling in the balance.

I got love ones on the block, Lord I ask you to save;
They are almost out of breath in a race to the grave.
Stacking paper high, serving meth to the tweeters,
Playing with their life to buy the latest sneakers.
See that jewelry shine, see that pit bull bark,
Do they even know that they are breaking your heart?

They're cold at the core, hunting one big score,
But you made them, God, for oh so much more.
They're soon to be dead or property of the state,
Having thrown away the life they don't appreciate.
Mama can't reach 'em, blind as they can be;
Open their eyes for a moment, Lord, and let them see.

PROTECT ME FROM MY ENEMIES

Lord, protect me from those who don't mean no good;
They creeping through the back streets of my hood.
Sometimes it's a fake homie whose smile is a mask,
Asking questions that he really has no business to ask.
Lord, protect me from those who don't mean me
   no good;
The ones who said, "I can't" when they really could.
Lord, protect me from enemies in the world that I roam;
From those who call my family when they know
   I'm not home.
Lord, protect me from those who don't mean no good;
They creeping through the back streets of my hood.

PRAYER BEFORE A KILLER'S TEMPER IS LOST

Lord, they messing with me but I'm about that action;
I'll leave their behind reclined in traction.
I'm a soldier at war, you know I'm hard core.
I'm no stranger to bringing the blood and the gore.
Acid rain, I'm half way insane.
If they step to me, I'm going to bring the pain.
Lord, only you know how many people I've killed;
Each one a step to the name that I built.
But like St. Paul, on the road you found me;
I bowed my knee, you wrapped your arms around me.
I was real about my repentance
So I got that pardon from that eternal sentence.
But now, Jesus, fools out here trying to unleash
The old me, the wild, chest-pounding beast;
And truly I'm about to show them something.
Go get that thang, thang and commence to dumpin',
But God, I know one thing and that's if I flash,
I'm gonna turn my future into molten ash.
So Savior, Savior, cool me down;
I'm coughing up hate, I'm about to drown.
Lord, cool me down, Lord, cool me down,
Lord, cool me down, Lord, cool me down.

PRAYER FOR A LOST GENERATION

Bound together by blocks, colors, and hate,
Flat line from the cradle to the prison gate.
They don't forgive let alone forget;
Generational banging, centuries of regret.
Is it a form of insanity, if
You put your kids in the car and speed off a cliff?
Lord, we losing our sons and daughters;
Shooting out here over nickels and quarters.
My son hanging out the window with the quarter pound;
The future lowered down to a hole in the ground.
Oh God, have mercy on this ship of fools.
Back when banging and hustling used to have rules,
Before you snitch you would pull your bid
And you wouldn't pull a gat out in front of no kids.
But those brothers on the corner sipping Crown Royal
Ain't loyal and they got no respect for the soil.
Lord, I ain't telling you something you don't know;
Their eyes got that glow, from sniffing that blow.
Lord, I'm talking in circles, but you understand.
If we don't change, where will we land?

PRAYER OF THANKS FOR THE TIME I MISSED

I wasn't with the B.S. that homeboy was yapping;
My emotions escaped and I started to clapping.
I slapped in a clip and then I aimed my gun
At the small of his back and he started to run.
I was so angry that my hands start to shaking;
I brought the fire and he brought the bacon.
As he ran away, I thought this was strange:
How could I miss three times from point blank range?
Is he bulletproof? Why he ain't dropped?
I started chasing the fool and then I stopped.
It's almost like you were saying, "Hold the phone;
The life you save here will be your own."
When he was dissing me it all went black,
But when you spoke, God, my mind came back.
Grim reaper got a hammer and he got a sickle
And I would have had to do that whole deuce
    and a nickel.
Thank you, God, 'cause you're in control;
That's one more less thing weighing on my soul.
Thank the Lord that I came out of that daze;
One more chance, I got to change to my ways.

A FOOL'S PRAYER

They say a leopard can't change a spot,
So, I'm waiting on the corner for the coroner's cot.
You see, I got these rocks loaded in my mouth
And when I die, you know I'm headed
    straight down south.
Ain't no thug mansion for us ghetto outlawz;
When I die, bury me in my fire-proof drawers.
I was a stone cold killer and a money go getter;
I blamed mama and the block, but really I knew better.
One day a pack of hyenas might catch me slippin',
Or I'll catch a hot one from a fool that's trippin'.
One day the po-po is going to run my plates,
And back I'll go again through them iron gates.
Teacher said I was smart but I really am not;
Or would I stand in the spot waiting to get got?
Lord, this is the ghetto hymn that I be hummin';
Hold on a second, I see a customer coming.

COMING DOWN FROM A HIGH PRAYER

My teeth are grit.
I'm trying to get lit.
I'd trade my soul for just one more hit.
I'm sweating.
My pulse is jetting.
See I got this internal Armageddon.
Some call it the thirst.
Can the curse be reversed?
Or will it fill my bones till I ride in a hearse?
That first hit was my downfall —
Lost family, friends, bank book, and all.
See me on my knees as I crawl.
You're the only one left who will answer my call.
Oh God, here I lay and here I pray;
Like a vampire tripping in the the light day.
Unleash my chains, two tons they weigh.
In the darkest hour, I'm trying to pray.
Hear me now my Higher Power;
Hide me in the safety of Your tower.

LORD, KILL THE GANGSTER IN ME

Like dust on a corpse, the remnants of death
Just rose to heaven on wings of my breath.
I'm 200 miles from the devil's reach,
But sometimes my past life slips out in my speech.
Lord, I am real about this, ain't no pretend,
Down to ride for your name to the very end.
Sometimes the old man slips in like he got a key,
So I plead, "Lord, kill the gangster in me."

PRAYER FOR AN ADDICTION TO STREET LIFE

The Life got me hooked bad;
I'm true to the game.
In the concrete jungle
Everyone knows my name.
It's all about eating;
I'm trying to get bread.
And God, you know,
I've laid bodies down dead.
I was born in hell with my flesh on fire,
So used to it now I don't even perspire.
Everybody got a plan, a plot, or scheme;
One last good run is the hustler's dream.
I had a dream last night they kicked down the door;
Made me get butt naked, laid me out on the floor.
They found bundles and a duffel bag with 10 grand;
Had my brother up there on the witness stand.
The judge sentenced me to the penitentiary,
With a release date for the next century.
That very next morning when I awoke,
I thought God was saying, "Fool, stop selling that coke."
Lord, you know me so well, it ain't even funny.
You know I'm addicted to the power and the money.
Father, from down here on my knees I pray;
Give a player the strength to just walk away.

PRAYER FOR ADDICTION TO OTHERS' OPINIONS

Lord, there are some prayers that I don't pray out loud;
I've got too much ego, I'm really just too proud.
If people heard this one that I'm about to speak,
They'd say, "I'm surprised. I didn't think Homestyle was that weak."
But Lord, I care too much what people think.
It's why I dress like I dress! It's why I drink what I drink!
It's why I fight or I'll shoot in half of a blink!
Lord, I care too much about what people think.
I hang around all day with people I hate;
They helped me get a number issued by the state.
In 9th grade I even dropped out of school,
Because it mattered so much who thought I was cool.
I've followed fools like a fish down a waterfall;
I am the pet who learned to run when the homies call.
I knew I was headed toward my demise,
But didn't want to be seen as weak in their eyes.
My future's gonna rinse right down the sink,
'Cause I care too much what people think.
But Lord, help me change;
But I can change.
Lord, help me change.

PRAYER OF CONFESSION FOR WAR AND BLOODSHED

You crafted us from the sand, the dirt, and the mud;
One humanity, one breath, one blood.
Flesh soft and pliant to the tender touch,
We ate figs, pomegranates, mint leaves, and such.
Then look at the Genesis genealogy table;
Cain's jealousy meant the end of Abel.
He broke the hearts of both his father and mother;
Blood cried from the ground when Cain
    slaughtered his brother.
Soon nation rose against nation,
    hood rose against hood;
We pulled a trigger on a brother and
    we thought it was good.
World War and children died in genocide;
We got you choking on the fumes and
    bleeding deep inside.
Our polluted thoughts rising up to heaven above;
We can quote the Bible but we can't spell love.
Lord, forgive what we have done to the ones we hated;
Blood is everywhere, the earth is saturated.
For starvation and despair we must beg your pardon;
Wash our minds in the rivers of Eden's garden.

PRAYER BEFORE A DRIVE-BY

Lord, see me on the corner staring in the skies;
I'm hard to recognize, hatred's in my eyes.
He said, she said, got them fools trippin';
Next thing you know there's bullets rippin'.
Caught 'em at the light, no second chance given.
Lord, everything I'm saying in this prayer is true;
I never lie to my lawyer, never lie to you.
Yes, my Lord and Savior, in you I trust,
But where we live is grimy, get back is a must.
I know where they stay, now I'm behind the wheel;
I see them fools on the corner, time to make it real.
Ten seconds left, I'm holding my breath;
Lord, do I turn right or do I turn left?

THE GANGSTA'S LAST PRAYER

Mama, I should have listened;
Now I'm ducked between two Chevys and I can hear
　the bullets whizzing.
Dead shells clicking on the pavement;
My connection to the game is my enslavement.
Should have bowed out last time I got knocked;
Now I'm jammed up on the block with my pistol cocked.
They reloading trying to send me death;
Just looked one bullet is all I got left.
I saw a light flash and then I heard a buzz;
Lord, tell Mama how sorry I was.

PRAYER FOR A GIRL ON THE TRACK

Oh God, how my heart does hurt;
See that child in the mini skirt?
The one on the corner in stiletto heels.
Leaning into the car with the gold rim wheels.
The one trying to get that player's cake up;
Wearing just a tad too much makeup.
'Cause last night she came in a Benjamin short;
He slapped my girl down in the street for sport.
She has spent too much time in the county cage,
And on her knees before men three times her age.
Some smell like cologne, others are dirty;
I wonder if my daughter will live to see thirty.
Oh God, who made the Red Sea part;
She's a slave to someone who has no heart.
Lord Jesus who hung on Calvary's tree,
Send a miracle, Lord, and set her free.

PRAYER FROM A PARENT IN THE GAME

Lord, the game is swallowing me,
But I got tiny footsteps following me.
As I bowed down to tie that little shoe,
I understand that they will do what I do.
Don't want my child to ever touch drugs,
Or be on the block trading slugs with thugs.
I want my child to turn the page,
To live a good life and then die of old age.
Lord, I know firsthand these words to be true;
My kids are gonna do what they see me do.
I want to visit this kid in college, not prison,
Influenced to do evil by my decision.
Coming from me this might sound odd,
But I want my child to walk with God.
Yes, from a hustler these words sound strange,
But God, for the sake of my child I must change.
So help me change,
Help me change.
Lord, help me change my ways.
Help me change,
Lord, help me change my ways.

PRAYER FOR THE HOMICIDE VICTIM'S FAMILY

We used to throw hands in one-on-ones,
But the fade is gone, we all got guns.
Too much pride, they can't take that whipping;
They'd rather pull a nine and stick that clip in.
But when the body drops and the smoke is clear,
You can read the eulogy in a Mama's tear.
Oh God in heaven, whom we love so much,
Reach down to the hood and give us your touch.
Killers out here shooting body parts;
Families left crushed, rows of broken hearts.
People feel they got to prove that they're tough;
Young people laid down over petty stuff.
Somebody's pride gets touched so they popping lead;
Now the dream's destroyed, somebody's child is dead.
God help the grandma whose wrinkled hands tremble
At the quiet hour when the beloved assemble.
When he was born, he was the family's pride and joy;
Never thought she'd be the one who would bury the boy.
Lord, bless the brother brimming over with hate,
Listening to all the calls to retaliate.
Lord, bless the mother and bless his dad
Whose rising days may forever be sad.

Lord, bless the deceased boy's little sister;
She was with him that day but I'm so glad they
 missed her.
Lord, in the moments that are so grim,
Touch all the people in this world who will cry for him.
He said, she said, ends in lead;
Dreams destroyed, somebody's child is dead.
Lord, night is so dark, will we ever see dawn?
God, help the victim's family to go on.

LORD, BLESS MY HOMIES

God, I ain't never had much in the way of bread,
But I got friends who stepped in or I'd be dead.
They ain't perfect but then again neither am I;
We were kids together, we'll be friends till we die.
We forgive and go on, 'cause it's whatever;
We eat the last scrap of food off the plate together.
Lord, bless the homies, bless and protect them;
Bless their families and those who love
    and respect them.

PRAYERS FOR CHILD SOLDIERS

In roadside formation, rebel killers saluted;
Deep in the villages, child soldiers recruited.
They try to unwind by doing long white lines;
Fathers digging deep in the diamond mines.
The world they inhabit is grim and dirty;
Consider yourself blessed if you live to see 30.
Somewhere the puppet master with golden rings
Sits behind the scenes pulling all the strings.
Back here in the states, some kids ain't kids,
In the gladiator camp pulling light year bids.
Have mercy on the 10-year-old on my block;
His mama strung out and he's slanging crack rock.
God bless those who come out the womb, hurled
Into a heartless, crime- and drug-infected world
Where hope is the first thing that gives in and dies.
In the land where hot bullets have no eyes,
Where death and fear fill the atmosphere,
Even the preacher's too afraid to come out here.
Amidst sirens, we were born with a need to eat;
Lord have mercy on the babies raised by the street.

PRAYER FOR DIRECTION

I'm at the crossroads without no map;
Am I headed toward treasure or is it a trap?
Lord, in the wilderness, where I can not see,
Whisper directions toward the light to me.
So many paths, so many choices,
So much advice, so many voices.
So many ways that seem to look right;
Lord, lead me straight through the dark of night.

PRAYER FOR A BELOVED CHILD

A traveler on the highway of truth;
She's made lemonade from the fountain of youth.
She's eternity in a single day;
She ain't hiding a single strand of gray.
So many lessons still yet to learn;
So many bridges yet to burn.
Future so bright clouds can't conceal
So many wins ahead for the highlight reel.
Oh God, give this child your vision,
Be in her every major decision.
Make her journey straight as Moses' rod,
Avoiding all the pretense and facade.
Let her remember her sisters and brothers;
Let her life mean something to you and to others.
So that when she enters her final days,
She'll find joy that she followed you in all your ways.
So that when the candle wick of life burns down,
She'll be ready to receive her crown.

PRAY FOR STRENGTH TO STAND TEMPTATION

Dazed in confusion, I got a nice contusion,
Last time I bit down on the devil's illusion.
The devil got victims, he ain't got friends,
So don't ride in the shotgun seat of his Benz.
His world-class lies pop your eyes in surprise,
You'll end up someone you can't even recognize.
One more chew and one more nibble,
Soon you'll be OD'ed on the devil's kibble.
He taking up a collection and plenty people giving it;
Sure there's hell, I talk to people that's living it.
No judgement here, we done fell for the charm;
Dancing in his mouse trap can cause you harm.
Lead me not, Lord, into the pool of temptation;
The trouble and the double-cross got inflation.
This might take a little more concentration;
Your entire empire for the sweet sensation.
Everything you worked for so hard
Falling down fast like a house of cards.
He always got a plot, a plan, or a scheme;
"Yeah, we can win if you get on my team.
The boss playa, he sure know how to come up,
Follow the leader, get that dollar sum up."
Hmmm, what's behind door number two?
It's ugly and almost it's too bad to be true.
He's clever, he's ruthless, and he's tricky;
He's impossible to avoid and his traps be sticky.
He ain't got pointy ears or a red jumpsuit;

He's a gangstafied pro all about the loot.
He's the personification of molten hate,
And chances are you won't see him until it's too late.
He'll tell you he's a myth, that he don't exist;
When you take a bite of the bait, it's so hard to resist.
He makes the pimps and players think they're
    too slick;
He can show up as a preacher laying hands on the sick.
Why you think Jesus told you pray, "Lead us not"?
The strength of God in this war is all a soldier got.
Without the armor of God, he ain't the one
    to be messed with;
In the desert he appeared and Jesus Christ got tested.
Satan lost that day but he lives by a code,
And he only stops by the side of the road to reload.
Are you marked by the blood? Choose the path
    of the light.
Superman don't play around with no kryptonite.
My fate is sealed so I can not yield;
I'm picking up the sword of the Lord and his shield.

GOOD MORNING, LORD

I still got the red river running warm in my veins;
I check the pulse then my wrists. I don't feel no chains.
Like the Red Sea crossed by an Israelite,
I survived the Middle Passage and been blessed
    with the light.
Like the Alaskan prince who once froze on a sled,
I been resurrected from the Land of the Dead.
Did you know that when you sleep your heart rate
    drops?
Breathing drops too, you pulse nearly stops.
Now I'm an eagle soaring out the family nest;
Thank God Almighty for a good night's rest.

PRAYER FOR INCARCERATED LOVED ONES

The house of steel and stone is weaponized;
Motives and intentions in stealth disguised.
Here you can't afford to ever look soft;
What you gonna do when the riot jumps off?
God Almighty will never, ever forsake you;
God's got your back so the stress won't break you.
Tears wet your pillow way past midnight;
Hungry 'cause your commissary looks light.
Here is a brand new definition of hell;
A wall with pictures of your kids in your prison cell.
Trying to sidestep the boredom and the deadly drama;
Thinking, I got to try to get back home to my mama.
God Almighty, who lives behind the stars,
I'm praying for my loved ones who be behind bars.
In the concrete jungle let them stand protected;
Let the hope in their souls be resurrected.
Oh God, you are the judge, that's what I was taught;
Many people did worse, they just ain't been caught.
Today bless my loved ones with mercy and grace;
Give them the strength as they run this race.
Protect them from evil, show them some good;
Work on their cases and bring 'em home to the hood.
Keep them safe tonight from the predator shark;
Be the light that shines when their world gets dark.

PRAYER FOR A TROUBLED MARRIAGE

I thought they were my rock but they really are flaky;
I said, "I do" too fast, the situation's shaky.
They be rapping to my friends and they got eyes
    that roam;
They make me so sick inside, I don't want
    to come home.
I would walk tomorrow and declare this dead,
But I remember the vows that I once said.
The joy we once shared has grown cold and rotten;
The laughter that knit two together, forgotten.
When my heart tells me go, give me strength to stay;
Help us work through this instead of walking away.
Lord, you joined us both together, man and wife;
God, we turn to you now, bless our marital life.

PRAYER THAT GOD USES ONE'S LIFE

Ain't it funny how the days are just slipping by?
Pages on the calendar just flipping by.
In your teens you think that it's whatever,
But then one day you realize you ain't got forever.
Got to make life count while you still in it,
'Cause all gold on Planet can't buy one more minute.
Use my life, dear God, until the glass is dry,
Until the moment that darkness invades my eye.
So that on the day of the eclipse on my setting sun,
You can look me in the face, nod and say, "Well done."

PRAYER FOR CONTROL OF THE TONGUE

Oh Lord, once again I've been hung,
Strung by the words that slipped from my tongue.
Before I open my mouth, I need to take a deep breath,
Because my tongue holds the power of life and death.
My tongue can create, my tongue can bust slugs,
My tongue can preach sermons, my tongue can
   sell drugs.
My tongue can cuss and lie or it can give praise;
My tongue can lead my children in the righteous ways.
My tongue can speak faith, my tongue can speak doubt.
Oh, Lord, help me live what I just figured out.
Before the dam bursts and the waters leak,
Help me, God, to think twice before I go to speak.

PRAYER FOR AN END TO AN UNHEALTHY ROMANTIC RELATIONSHIP

Savior, Savior, hold my hand;
I'm in lust with someone I just can't stand.
We ain't good together, I can do better;
The devil is not only smart, he's clever.
We are creating spiritual homicide;
The damage done here can't be denied.
I really wish that I could part from this,
But I'm sprung like a trampoline artist.
I'm in the spiritual E.R. yelling, "Flat line!"
I'm wasting my life, but, Lord, they're so fine.
My neck wrapped tight in a hangman's noose;
I'm struggling and kicking but I can't get loose.
My mind and my soul ripped apart by the schism;
What we really need here is an exorcism.
I've done paid all that I want to pay;
Lord give me the power to simply to walk away
From this love affair, the devil's lie,
That always leaves teardrops dripping from my eye.
Lord, bring the flaming sword and let it fly;
It's time to let this soul-tie die.

SOCIAL SERVICES LINE PRAYER

Lord, I'm in a bind, on another line,
In another office where they're so unkind.
They probe, disrespect, and harass me,
And when I speak they look right past me.
I wonder what in the world they are seeing,
And I know it's not me, I'm a human being.
I'm made in your image, resemble your form;
Your mighty power keeps my blood type warm.
You made my hair a distinctly beautiful grade;
I am tearfully, fearfully, wonderfully made.
I can keep my cool, I can smile and nod,
Because I know in my heart that I'm a child of God.
My life is yours and my soul has been set free;
Nothing they say or do can ever define me.

PRAYER THROUGH PHYSICAL PAIN

Lord, what is this stabbing me?
What is the awful sensation that's grabbing me?
I can feel the cold breath of the angel of doom;
I hold my breath when the doctor walks in the room.
My world is now a circus of needles and pills;
I got something going on medicine can't kill.
I got doubt in mind that won't leave me alone;
My eyes look through the dark clouds and I can
    see your throne.
Oh God, I envision the glow of your face,
And I ask to be touched once again with your grace.
Oh, my Creator, please squeeze my hand;
One minute at a time, Father help me to stand.
Lord, wrap your arms ever tightly around me;
Let your divine presence never cease to astound me.
I'm holding on to your words because I know
    they're true;
Journey with your child; God see me through.

PRAYER FOR THE UNDOCUMENTED

Lord, they ain't got a clue;
If they were in my sneakers what wouldn't they do?
Sure I came up here from the south;
I wanted to put bread in my baby's mouth.
I was led through the desert, I was thirsty for water;
All I could think of was my wife and my daughter.
Now I live with the threat of being thrown in a cage;
I'm busting my back for half the minimum wage.
America the beautiful, Cali the sweet;
They don't treat us so well but at least we can eat.
Just had a second child, a legal resident;
One day she may be the President.
Lord, I've given all that I can to the land of free;
Jesus, watch over my family and me.

PRAYER FOR BASIC NEEDS

Lord, my wallet's empty and I find myself quite short;
My rent is way past due and I owe child support.
I'm not one to pout, but my money has just run out;
Jesus born in the hood, you know what I'm talking 'bout.
I ain't asking for no jet, I don't need no Rolls,
But I surely need paper, the green kind that folds.
Looked in the fridge with dread, there was no
    butter or bread;
Not even no cold water, even the light bulb was dead.
I ain't got nothing left, just prayer plus faith and hope,
So I aim my eyes toward heaven and use
    faith's telescope.
Lord, this is your child; Would you please take heed?
You're the one I can depend on. Savior, meet my need.

PRAYER OF PRAISE

We say God is good all the time,
But when the road is tough to climb
And beneath my feet are flaming sands,
Oh God, it's hard to raise my hands.
Praise God when ribs are on your plate;
Praise God when that was PBJ and you ate.
Praise God when it's sunny and the sky is clear;
Praise God when there's rain in the atmosphere.
Praise God when you feel good and when you don't ;
Praise God when it goes well and when it won't.
Praise God. Praise God. Praise God. Praise God
    all the time.

PRAYER OF THANKS
FOR A FRIEND IN RECOVERY

I just saw my friend and she was sober
As the last leaf on a branch in late October.
I once saw her knocking at death's door;
Today she's rising, watch that eagle soar!
One day at a time and one hour by hour,
Hand in hand with the Higher Power.
Let freedom ring, said Dr. King;
Sobriety is really such a wonderful thing.

LORD, LET ME REST

Lord, I've been wandering barefoot through
    deserts and valleys;
Drifting through hoods, facing devils in valleys.
I've fought the forces of hell for immortal souls;
Had to walk barefoot over burning coals.
Hollering the Gospel in a world so dark;
Feeding homeless friends who live in the park.
Me and the crew faced the devil's tanks;
When it was done there was no one to say thanks.
Your yoke is easy and your burden is light,
But the faces of lost people come to visit at night.
The fight waxes hard as the world grows colder;
Lord, let me rest my head on your shoulder.
I'm flawed and frail but my passion is true;
Give me grace for the race as I run it with you.
Sometimes, even one step at a time is a test;
Lord, I'm exhausted; let your servant rest.

IF THIS IS REAL

If this is real, then second birth
Means you are the Sun and I am the Earth.
Rotating around the fire day and night,
My existence depends on absorbing Your light.
If this is real, then what does it cost
To be rescued by blood on Golgotha's cross?
If this is real, like water or air,
How deep must I go?
How much should I share?

PRISON INDUSTRIAL COMPLEX PRAYER

Shackled in court, ready to face my doom;
Stand when the judge walks in the room.
Civics lesson time in the land of free;
Everybody stood up for the judge but me.
Grandma stared at me, she was crying;
It hurt so bad, inside I was dying.
The judge shook his head, he was set to trip;
He banged the gavel and curled his lip.
He said, "Son, you should have taken the plea;
Can't you see, in two years you'd have been set free?"
"First, Sir," I said, "I am not your son,
Because if I was, we would both see justice done."
Equality in court is just a fairy tale;
I don't have a job, I'm too poor to make bail.
Said, "Excuse me, please let me say, Your Honor,
I was raised in a pool full of hungry piranhas,
And where I was born if you wanted respect,
You learned early that it came at the end of a tech.
It was a jungle without elephants and monkeys,
Just killers, cutthroats, thieves, and junkies.
I stand before you here, Sir, without fear,
'Cause my kindergarten teacher said I'd end up here."
This is the great house of sucker bets and threats,
Where the state gets rich off poor folks' debts.
Only God can judge me, so let me stop and pray,
Lord, the system's corrupt and it's been that way.

This evil man hides behind a long, black robe,
So he can treat poor people like the devil did Job.
They snatched us up straight off of the block;
They flip us for a come up like we was crack rock.
Like captured slaves, we were marched off at the dock,
Then traded on Wall Street as prison stock.
Lord, sometimes I have to wonder what comes next?
We're chained to the prison industrial complex.
The emancipation proclamation
Freed the dark people in this nation.
Oh God, shut down the penitentiary;
It's slavery in the 21st century.

GRACE BEFORE MEALS

Steam is rising from the food I'm about to eat:
Vegetables, starches, fruit, and meat.
Bless now Lord this t-bone steak;
Forgive me for my great mistake:
To eat the food that I never planted,
To take what's on this plate for granted.
As I pick my knife and fork to carve,
I give no thought to those who starve.
With no access to clean, fresh water,
Civil war bullets causing great slaughter.
Just as sure as this prayer is lyrical,
The way we eat in the States is a miracle.

PRAYER WHEN LIFE IS HARD

I walked the desert all through the night,
Landed at the castle at the crack of light.
Lord, hear my groan 'cause my knuckles are sore;
I been here since dawn, there's blood on the door.
Tumbleweeds rolling across the plains;
Vegetation dead, three years without rains.
So hungry for change, I'm about to pass out;
I'm all alone but still surrounded by doubt.
Lord, I know you've got me in your scope;
Help me this day to hold on to hope.
You are refuge for me in this barren land;
I lay my life before you; Lord, help me stand.

PRAYER FOR AMERICA'S OPPRESSED

Strange fruit hanging from a southern tree;
Sweaty hands grip bars praying to be free.
And my insurance won't pay the cost of my healing;
My sister can't climb through the plexiglass ceiling.
The judge banged the gavel down and he cussed,
And his courtroom circus is so unjust.
That's why I fold my hands together to pray;
Lord, hear these words from my lips of clay.
Once the Hebrew children begged to be free;
You waved your hand and parted the sea.
Today I pray for those trapped in the prison hole;
Wrap your arms around some broken soul.
In your house, church is always in session;
Give strength to those who fight oppression.

FORGIVE ME, LORD

Forgive me, Lord, I had good intentions;
The wrong I've done defies dimensions.
Measured on a human scale,
I'm like a seed swallowed deep inside a whale.
Lost at sea, in the depths of the ocean,
Dark like Jonah churning in slow motion.
Forgive me, Lord, for all my transgressions;
Jesus, be my priest, hear my confessions.

PRAYER FOR FAITH

When the clouds are thick and the sun is dim,
And friends ask, "Why do you trust in Him?"
When the haters shake their heads at my fall,
When family won't accept my calls,
Your word is still right, your path is true,
And I will continue to trust in you.

PRAYER FOR THE SEXUALLY ABUSED

Like a child with scars so hard to heal,
The hunter clubbed the baby seal.
Mama, your words were stainless steel;
How could I know the boogie man was real?
The child had no words, face down in a pillow,
His face was rough and scratched like Brillo.
Just how much pain can one child take?
How much suffering, how much heartache?
Oh God, now that your child is grown,
Heal every heartache, hear every moan.
Wrap this child up in your amazing grace;
Kiss every tear from off of their face.
And Lord, when the brutal memories come,
Protect your child from the evil one.

PRAYER FOR THE HOMELESS

Lord, I need to say something, but it's hard to pray it;
Hard times don't even begin to say it.
I was on the ave, I just walked past Ray;
He looked at me and said, "Reverend, pray."
He's got no where to lay his head;
The approach of the night sky brings him dread.
God please bless the homeless, those with
   nowhere to go;
Those whose bones tremble whenever cold winds blow.
Oh Lord, please bless the homeless people
   living in the street,
Nowhere to lay their heads and not very much to eat.
God, have mercy;
God, have mercy;
God, have mercy
On the homeless.
God, have mercy;
God, have mercy;
God, have mercy
On those who have no home.

PRAYER FOR THE BROKEN HEARTED

How could they do this?
I've just been kissed by Judas!
Tell me, oh God, how will I get through this?
I've been cast aside
And I've been betrayed;
Lord, I can hardly talk,
My heart has been slayed.
But you're close to the broken,
To the wounded in spirit;
When I cry from my soul,
I know you'll hear it.
Help me go on, Jesus, one day at a time;
There are valleys ahead
And mountains to climb.
My heart been shredded and torn;
I ain't hurt so bad since the day I was born.
Inside I feel like I want to die;
I see the moon turn to blood in the sky.
Even my closest friends can't feel me;
Lord God, you alone are able to heal me.
My heart is broken, but you can heal me.
Heal me, Lord. Heal me.

PRAYER FOR A DEEPER WALK

My soul's bone dry, I got a spiritual leak,
Ain't prayed or read your word this week.
When I should have been seeking the Great Unseen,
I was hypnotized by the computer screen.
Do I need to wait till all hell breaks loose,
When devil tries to stick my head in a noose,
To awaken to your presence all around me?
But the truth is Lord, every since you found me,
Miracles and wonders surround me.
I can't let the lethargy come to drown me,
Lord, I stretch forth my hands to your mighty throne.
Now I'm moonwalking in the holy zone,
No longer stressed, my sins I've confessed.
Now I walk around clothed in your righteousness.
No more prayer time playing or empty word saying,
Let my heart reflect on what my lips are saying.

PRISONER'S PRAYER

I was a boss player in a high stakes game,
And when I lost, they took away my name.
I should have walked through life somewhat humbler,
Now the state knows me as a prison number.
My pay to play lawyer done lost my case,
Now my home is an 8- by 6-foot space.
In this petri dish of molten insanity,
They suspend your membership card to humanity.
Lord get my front, my sides and my back,
Where death can come from eye contact.
Who do I trust when the lines get blurred?
My faith rests in your Holy Word.

PRAYER FOR THE CHILDREN

Oh God, we send prayers for the kids who got it tough;
They got parents who care but not quite enough.
They know more than they should at their
    age and stage,
Like blind mice let loose in a lion cage.
They have eyes that sparkle with light and wonder,
In a hurricane waiting to take them under.
Oh God, let your mercy shine down on the kids
With daddies locked away doing double-digit bids.
They go to schools that would have made
    Einstein drop out,
And made the late Marvin Gaye wanna holler
    and shout.
Have mercy on the kids, Lord, love and keep
    them strong
Where the nights are dark and the road is long.

BACKSLIDER'S PRAYER

Lord, the scent of smoke is on my clothes;
Brimstone floats straight up my nose.
I'm an outlaw, I guess you can call me a rider;
I am also known to your throne as "backslider."
I was headed head high for Heaven's riches,
But got sidetracked and fell down into ditches.
God, once I drank from your holy fountain ,
Now, I'm a rolling stone, tumbling down a mountain.
I had victory in hand but I dropped it all;
Forgive and restore me, hear when I call.

GOOD MORNING, LORD

Thank you, God, for your presence within,
To feel the blessing of the sun caressing my skin.
Thank you, Lord Jesus Christ, for another day;
Let me reflect your glory as I go my way.

GOOD NIGHT, LORD

Thank you tonight for today's blessings,
The good, the bad, and all the life lessons.
Thank you for your love that has proven so deep;
Please watch over my family as we drift off to sleep.

HEAL MY NIGHTMARES PRAYER

Lord, please stop the evil that seems to seep
Deep in my soul and when I sleep.
Protect me from the midnight hour attack
That comes when I'm unconscious and can't fight back.
Oh God, I cast all of my troubles and my cares on you,
Even when I am asleep, Lord, please see me through.
As I close my eyes, place a hand on my brow;
I cast my soul in your mighty hands right now.

PRAYER FROM THE PIT OF DEPRESSION

Lord, I lay in my sheets like a frog in a log,
Afraid to peek out, I can't see in the fog.
I'm broken, I'm crushed, Lord God, and I'm bleeding;
It's a touch from you now that I'm needing.
I gotta trust your heart when I can't see your hand;
Pick me up, Lord Jesus, and help me stand.
Savior, please help me to make this climb.
Reach through eternity and into time
When my brain has turned to solid lead.
Father, kiss your child's forehead;
Tell the raging waters to calm and cease;
Whisper to my spirit sweet words of peace.

PRAYER FOR A JOB

God, Creator, Almighty Being;
Lord who exists light years beyond our seeing.
To the Alpha and Omega to whom I pray
To the possessor of the keys to Judgement Day.
God, there simply is no way to explain
The mysterious ways that you've made it rain.
For this passenger on the Holy Ghost Tour,
I've been stretched tight with what I've had to endure.
Not long ago, my paycheck stopped;
The safety net popped, income level got chopped.
The Psalm said the righteous are never forsaken,
But mouths at home expect me to bring back bacon.
Tomorrow there's a great job interview;
Lord, I've done what I can, now please do what you do.
Tell Heaven's post office to send down the mail;
I got gangsta faith, I know you can not fail.

LORD, BLESS MY CHILDREN

Lord, sometimes I think that you saved me
So I could do good for the children you gave me.
I could have caught that sentence, could caught
   those slugs,
Or OD'd one night from using all of those drugs.
Oh God, keep my children in good health;
Grant them a good education and a portion of wealth.
When they kneel down to pray, God hear their voices;
When they're away from me, let them make
   good choices.
God, bless my kids, may we forever be tight;
Show me how to love them, give me insight.

PRAYER FOR PEOPLE OF COLOR

Lord, I came into the world with a legal conviction;
My skin was my sin and then it spread to my diction.
So when I go to the mall I get these funny looks;
White women look scared and clutch their pocket books.
Security follows me around the store,
And they just look down when I ask them,
  "What is this for?"
If I get arrested, they'll try their best to burn me,
'Cause we ain't got the bread to pay no real attorney.
Lord being brown or black has been a trip,
Since we crossed the border or boarded the ship.
I say, "Fight The Power" as I raise my fist;
They say it's in my mind, racism don't exist.
Lord, help me fight for justice till my moment of death;
Let me die with "freedom" whispered on my breath.

LORD, HELP ME BE STILL

Just like water rose with power from Moses' rod,
Empower me in your presence when I am still, God.
I've been moving too fast, I've been doing too much;
Let me be still in prayer as I wait for your touch.

PRAYER FOR THE HEALING OF A BROKEN HEART

Toss me off a roof top and let me fall,
But the pain of a broken heart is worst of all.
Take out a hammer and smash my fingers;
One day I'll forget but a broken heart lingers.
Been in the hospital about to lose my life,
And I been stabbed in the back but not with a knife.
Looking back the hospital stay is just a blur,
But every day I wake, I still think about her.
Heal me, Lord, take away this sense of loss;
Let the pain melt away as I follow the cross.
Oh God, heal me, Savior, let me go on;
Tears endure for the night but I believe for the dawn.

PRAYER FOR A PLACE TO STAY

Oh God, rescue me from the homeless zone;
Let me find a bed that I call my very own.
God, I'm so tired of being broken and poor;
Please grant me a key that turns in a door.
Lord send help to me, let me follow through;
When you do this for me, I'll give glory to you.

PRAYER FOR SELFLESSNESS

God, please give me a heart that thinks of others,
Hungry children, and homeless mothers,
People in faraway lands overseas
Who live in squalor and fight infectious disease.
God, give me a heart that thinks of others,
That prays for incarcerated sisters and brothers.
A heart with hands that does what it can
For those who dance in hot grease in the frying pan.
Lord, as I worship you here beneath the steeple,
Give me a heart for homeless people.
The people forced to pay the heaviest toll,
For being poor makes you an invisible soul.

PRAYER FOR A LOVED ONE ON DRUGS

Lord, I kneel before you and I bow my head;
I have a loved one in the Land of the Living Dead.
They ignore more pleas because they love to get high;
Every parting hug could be the last goodbye.
I'm afraid that they are soon to be deceased;
They are caught in the teeth of the chemical beast.
I pray, I beg, I rave, and I rant;
Now step in, God, 'cause you can do what I can't.
Oh God, I love (person's name) so very much;
Free (person's name) from the devil's clutch.

PRAYER THAT GOD USES ONE'S LIFE

Ain't it funny how the days are just slipping by?
Pages on the calendar just flipping by.
In your teens you think that it's whatever,
But then one day you realize you ain't got forever.
Got to make life count while you still in it,
'Cause all the gold on Planet can't buy one more minute.
Use my life, dear God, until the glass is dry,
Until the moment that darkness invades my eye.
So that on the day of the eclipse on my setting sun,
You can look me in the face, nod and say, "Well done."

PRAYER BEFORE FACING A MEAN PERSON

Her eyes are dead, her viewpoint slanted;
Her heart is cold like a burned out planet.
And as sure as I'm rhyming as I call on the Lord,
She just cut me six ways with the tip of her sword.
Not the one made of steel but the one in the lips;
She's a soldier of doom rocking extra clips.
And as soon as I move to turn the other cheek,
She wanna pull the shank and play hide and seek.
But I'm gonna stand still though 'cause this is my test,
And Lord Jesus Christ you are my bullet proof vest.
I know the Lord gonna hear my cry when I call;
Your word is propping me up and I will not fall.
I'm going to trust in the Lord for the rest of my days,
Till she hear Santana and changes her ways.
I got a shield of faith to stop a flaming arrow;
The road I'm taking is straight and narrow.

PRAYER IN A MOMENT OF FEAR

A number came up on my phone that caused
    me to tremble;
I had to stop and give my thoughts a chance
    to assemble.
It was the moment I feared, it blew my natural mind;
If I picked up the line I knew the trouble I'd find.
You say that perfect love will cast out all fear;
Nothing strange about that, I hear you loud and clear.
God, I'm staring up at you, gazing through the ceiling;
Let my faith in you overcome these feelings
Of doubt and worry, anxiety and dread,
Circling like bees buzzing around my in head.
Fear got me stuck, I can't get out bed;
I got a choice to worry or to trust you instead.
I'm going to sit in your peace, and I refuse to doubt;
I lay this burden on you, Lord, come work this out.
Nothing in my situation is out of your reach;
You created the world with a few words of speech.

PRAYER FOR RENT MONEY

It's the first of the month and the rent is due.
Who can I turn to, Almighty God, but you?
I touched the light switch but I'm still in the dark;
Reality for me is now quite stark.
I should have kept that payment agreement;
The world is hard like rocks in the cement.
I got many gifts, Lord, so many talents,
But my bank account got a negative balance.
Sometimes I feel like I want to jump overboard,
But the Word tells me I got to wait on the Lord.
I'm going through hell and I feel frustrated,
But some day I'll be oh so glad that I waited.
Almighty One, please supply my pressing need,
'Cause I got faith the size of a mustard seed.
The life of faith truly ain't for the soft;
I'm down to ride with you till the wheels fall off.

PRAYER FOR THE STRENGTH TO FORGIVE FAMILY

My soul is just seething with hate;
I need a mind cleanse to rehabilitate.
I didn't ask to be here, but here I be;
They should have looked out and protected me
From the evil that seeped in the streets of the hood;
These fools made choices against my good.
I go to see them Christmas and Thanksgiving,
But in my book they stand before me unforgiven.
They share the blame for the path I chose;
I ain't got no love because my heart is froze.
But, Lord God, let me chill since this is prayer;
You know that I can't just leave it there.
"Lord, please forgive me" are the words I pray
At the conclusion of every single day.
My sins be ugly, I be thinking wrong,
But at the end of the day, it's the same old song.
You died alone on Calvary's tree;
You shed your blood and you forgave me.
Hinging all that on one condition;
That I, too, forgive — but, God, that's a mission.
It took the shedding of blood to release my debt;
Still, God, I can't forgive and I can't forget.
It's something that can't be done on my own;
Lord, give me the strength to just leave it alone.

WHY?

Missiles whistle over the desert in the dead of night,
People blown to bits who couldn't put up a fight.
Children and old folks face an ugly end
And Lord I even gon' sit here and try to pretend.
I got some rage in my soul Lord as I look to you;
This is the reason many don't even think
   that you're true.
Because if there is a God and God has all power,
Where were you when folks cried out in the
   missile shower,
As they ran for the church and as they called
   your name?
Why you ain't do nothing when the missiles came?
Why, that's a question draped high in the sky.
I've seen senseless tragedy, God, tell me why
I can never get my foot off the bottom rung.
My nephew was a good kid and now he's strung;
Got a pink slip on pay day, now that stung.
And of course I'm gonna ask, why do the good
   die young?
Why must the poor always take the loss?
Why you turn your head from Jesus on the cross?
My sister got stabbed, they doused her in gasoline,
Blood was splashed over the murder scene.
Lord as she stared into the eyes of the angel of death,
What was the last thing word on her dying breath?
Why's the word deeper than the deepest seas,
We just have to trust God with some mysteries.

PRAYER FROM ONE WHO'S BEEN FORGIVEN

Wolves in the alley gave me the bum rush;
I fell to the pavement and felt my bones crush.
Couldn't have seen this coming in a
    Stephen King dream.
I used to run the streets day and night
    with my thug life team.
I was loyal to the fam so how could they betray me?
Caught me slipping one night and they tried to slay me.
I looked for a faithful friend but found none,
Except one, Jesus Christ, the Lord God's Son.
Jesus knows what it was like to be betrayed
    and rejected;
He conquered death and the grave and was resurrected.
Through blood and faith with God I am now connected;
Through grace alone was this homie selected.
In the soil of my soul I feel Christ's love grow;
With eternal life essence I will always glow.
Christ will never turn away, never forsake me;
If I mess up somewhere, He never gonna shake me.
Trying to separate God from His son or daughter
Is like trying to take away the wet taste from water.
Think for a minute, it just can't be done;
That's why I'm hanging to the sleeve of God's only Son.

PRAYER FOR A DOMESTIC VIOLENCE SURVIVOR

The promises and kisses must be the worse
Than the rage at 30 decibels when they curse.
In the hospital when you're trying to mend
They say, "That's last time, I'll never do it again."
He transforms like Michael Jackson in Thriller
And next time there's a chance that he just might kill her.
Lord, there's altogether too much airtight silence
Around the dreaded disease called domestic violence.
Last week when the fellas all went out bowling,
I looked at my homie and his eye was swollen.
God give wisdom to those who linger and doubt,
And if they need to take it, show them the way out.
Being in love won't get you stomped, kicked, or bit,
And if you ain't wearing gloves it ain't fun to be hit.
Lord, protect the one whose self esteem is shot
From long time abuse from one whose temper is hot.
Lord, grant common sense to one who doesn't believe
That if you're abused, then it's best you should leave.
Lord, protect those burdened with a heavy load;
Let 'em know there will be freedom if they cross
   the road.

THE BELIEVER'S PRAYER

Phillip said out loud, "Can anything good…"
Come straight out of the Nazareth hood?
We followed you from the womb to the tomb,
To the resurrected appearance in the upper room.
In the beginning, we followed the star;
We heard your voice and we believe who you are.
In the age of science, people think it odd
That true believers see you as the Son of God.
Lord, we done made our eternal decision;
Now we're deep in the streets, playing our position.
We picked up a cross, we counted the cost;
Now we're bread, water, and life to the lost.
We're in the struggle, waist-deep for God's only Son;
Lord, receive our souls when this life is done.

ABOUT THE AUTHOR

Reverend Harry Williams was born in Brooklyn, New York. He was raised in Asbury Park, NJ. Oakland, CA has been his home since 2002. He holds a B.A. from Kean University, Union, NJ, and an M.Div. from Palmer Theological Seminary, Wayne, PA. He preaches the Gospel and serves as a well-respected community activist in the San Francisco Bay Area.

Follow Harry Williams (aka O.G. Rev) online:
Instagram: OG.rev510
Twitter: @revharry1
Facebook: facebook.com/harry.l.williams.12

www.IAmOGRev.com
whenthestruggleisrealOG@gmail.com

**GOD IS MERCIFUL.
LOOK UP!**

Made in the USA
Monee, IL
07 April 2021